NEBRASKA

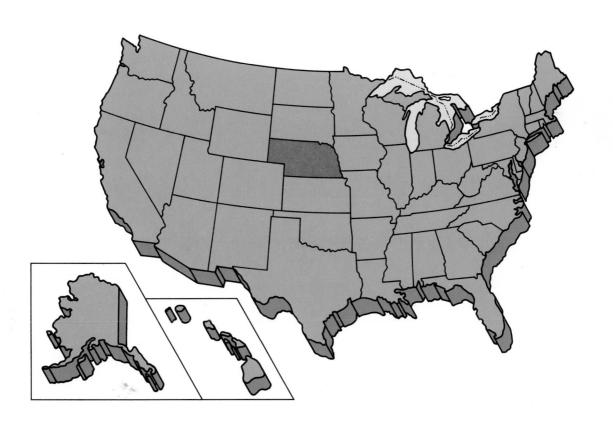

NEBRASKA

A.P. Porter

Lerner Publications Company

LIBRARY OF CONGRESS
CATALOGING-IN-PUBLICATION DATA
Porter, A. P.
        Nebraska / A. P. Porter.
            p.   cm. — (Hello USA)
        Includes index.
        Summary: Introduces the geography, history, people, industries, and other highlights of Nebraska.
        ISBN 0-8225-2708-1 (lib. bdg.)
        1. Nebraska—Juvenile literature.
    [1. Nebraska.] I. Title. II. Series.
    F666.3.P67 1991
    978.2—dc20   90-13534
                                            CIP
                                             AC

Cover photograph courtesy of National Park Service.

The glossary that begins on page 68 gives definitions of words shown in **bold type** in the text.

Manufactured in the United States of America

1 2 3 4 5 6 7 8 9 10 99 98 97 96 95 94 93 92 91

 This book is printed on acid-free, recyclable paper.

CONTENTS

Did You Know . . . ?

☐ Lincoln, Nebraska, is home to the world's only museum of roller skating.

☐ The largest planted forest in the United States is in Nebraska. Covering 22,000 acres (8,910 hectares), the trees are part of the Nebraska National Forest.

The National Museum of Roller Skating honors Fred Murree, a professional skater and Pawnee Indian from Nebraska. Murree performed on skates until he was 82 years old!

Before it was the Cornhusker State, Nebraska was called the Bug-eating State because of its many nighthawks, which eat insects.

The world's first rodeo was held at North Platte, Nebraska, in July 1882 and starred its founder, William Frederick "Buffalo Bill" Cody.

The world's largest fossil of a woolly mammoth was found in Nebraska. It is 13 feet 4 inches (4.1 meters) high.

Prairie grasses *(above)* grow in Nebraska's Rainwater Basin. On the Platte River *(facing page)*, sandhill cranes rest before flying to their summer homes in Canada.

8

A Trip Around the State

Most of Nebraska, four-fifths, is part of the Great Plains—a huge, flat region in central North America. Before people lived on the earth, the Great Plains were the floor of a shallow sea that formed when glaciers in the area melted.

Long after the sea dried up, the Oto Indians named the river that crossed through the region *nebrathka,* which means "flat water." French explorers used their word for "flat" when they called that flat water the Platte River.

Now the wide, flat Platte River oozes slowly eastward through Nebraska farmland, collecting the flow of the Loup and Elkhorn rivers along the way. Eventually the Platte flows into the Missouri River, which borders Nebraska on the east. The Niobrara, Republican, and Big Blue rivers also find their way into the Missouri.

Across the Missouri River are the states of Missouri and Iowa. To Nebraska's north is South Dakota, and Wyoming is to the west. Colorado takes a chunk out of Nebraska's southwestern corner. Kansas lies to the south.

Two land regions—the Till Plains and the Great Plains—make up Nebraska. Both regions are considered **prairie**, or grassland, but the Till Plains get more rain and are more fertile than the Great Plains.

The Till Plains stretch along the Missouri River, covering one-fifth of the state. **Glaciers**—snow and ice packed up to a mile high—once inched across this region in eastern Nebraska. They dragged particles of clay, sand, and rock along the ground. Called **till**, the debris was strewn across the Till Plains by the glaciers.

Over time, **loess** (windblown dust) combined with the till to form the rich soil that feeds prairie grasses on the Till Plains. Till and loess also have made the Till Plains excellent for growing crops.

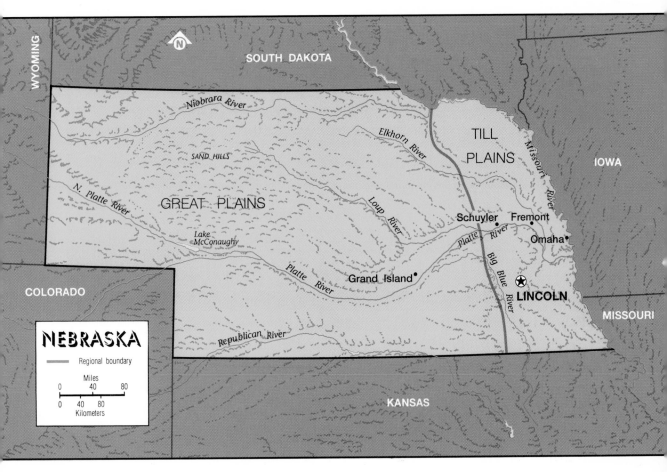

11

Nebraska's Sand Hills stretch for miles and miles.

West of the Till Plains, the mostly treeless Great Plains extend westward for more than 400 miles (644 kilometers)—all the way into Wyoming and Colorado. Grazing cattle and fields of wheat are common sights on the Great Plains.

Hills of sand roll through the center of Nebraska's Great Plains region. Called the Sand Hills, this section is the largest area of sand dunes in the United States. Unlike most other dunes, the Sand Hills are covered with grasses that hold the sand in place. The rich grasses and many streams of the Sand Hills make the area especially good for grazing cattle.

Across the state, dams have been built on rivers to collect water for **hydropower**. The water is then released to turn wheels that generate electricity. Water held back by the dams creates several of Nebraska's lakes, including Lake McConaughy, the state's biggest. These lakes can also be used to collect floodwaters, which can be released slowly into rivers so they won't flood homes and farms.

Nebraska's largest waterfall, Snake River Falls, is in the Sand Hills.

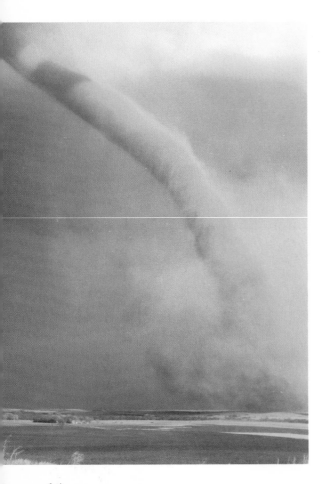

A tornado strikes a field, raising a huge dust cloud. These spiraling windstorms can sweep across the land at 60 miles (97 kilometers) per hour.

Floods are a common threat in Nebraska, where blizzards, hailstorms, and tornadoes lash the plains and prairies most years. At other times, however, **droughts,** or prolonged dry spells, endanger the state's crops and cattle. Weather in Nebraska swings from hot summers to cold winters. Temperatures average 76° F (25° C) in July and 23° F (−5° C) in January.

Snow frosts the branches of Nebraska's trees in winter.

When European explorers passed through Nebraska, they saw few trees in the region. Now the Nebraska National Forest is the largest planted forest in the United States. Cottonwood, oak, willow, linden, and ash trees all grow well in Nebraska, especially along riverbanks. Still, only 2 percent of the state is wooded.

Patches of wildflowers splash bright colors across these rocks in southwestern Nebraska.

Bluestem and other tall prairie grasses grow wild in eastern Nebraska. Grama and buffalo grass need little rain and grow mostly in the west, where less than 18 inches (46 centimeters) of rain fall each year.

In eastern Nebraska, which gets about 27 inches (69 cm) of rain most years, phlox, violets, and evening primroses greet each spring. Wildflowers such as spiderworts, wild roses, poppies, and blue flags grow well all over the state during the hot summers.

Mule deer, coyotes, skunks, raccoons, and prairie dogs are some of the wild animals found in Nebras-

16

ka. Ducks, geese, pheasants, quail, and cranes nest mainly in the wet **marshlands** of the Rainwater Basin near the Platte River.

At one time, millions of bison (buffalo) roamed the Great Plains in Nebraska and other states. Almost all of these animals were killed by white hunters in the late 1800s. Now buffalo are protected on game preserves.

The black-tailed prairie dog (above) **and the bull elk** (right) **make their homes on Nebraska's prairie.**

Nebraska's Story

About 10,000 years ago, when the first humans arrived in what later became Nebraska, the region was a green plain. Big animals such as 8-foot (2.4-m) moose, sloths the size of elephants, and 14-foot (4.3-m) woolly mammoths ate plants. Meat eaters included the short-faced bear, the dire wolf, and teratorns, birds with 15-foot (4.6-m) wing-spans.

Woolly mammoths roamed Nebraska more than 10,000 years ago. They had tusks that sometimes grew to be 13 feet (4 meters) long. That's twice the size of a tall person!

For centuries, millions of bison roamed the grasslands of the Great Plains.

Early Native Americans, or Indians, of the Great Plains lived in small groups and moved several times a year. Hunters ambushed bison near water holes or drove them over cliffs, killing dozens of animals at a time. The people ate the flesh and used the rest of the animal parts for clothing, shelter, and tools.

By A.D. 1200, some American Indians were growing squash, beans, and corn in what became Nebraska. They also traded furs, hides, and dried meat. Giant dust storms in the 1400s may have forced these people out of the area.

But other groups found their way onto the Great Plains. For centuries the Pawnee farmed and hunted the land that became Nebraska. The Pawnee, like other Indian tribes, had no written language. For their history they relied on storytellers, who told the next generations about the tribe's past and added important events from their own lifetimes.

Indians fitted their spears and arrows with stone points to hunt deer, bear, and bison.

By the 1600s, the Oto, Ponca, Omaha, and Iowa Indians had moved to what is now eastern Nebraska. They had come from farther east to get away from their enemies and to find food. Like the Pawnee, these newcomers lived in earthen houses and farmed during the summer. The rest of the year they followed herds of bison.

In what became western Nebraska, the Plains Apache and the Dakota Sioux led a different life-style. Rather than farming the land in one place, they spent most of the year on the move, hunting game and gathering wild plants for food.

Hush Little Baby

Often on the move, western Plains Indians followed different customs than eastern Plains Indians. For example, the Dakota Sioux kept strict rules of behavior. Parents taught their children from birth never to cry, because a crying child could betray the group to its enemies. Lots of helpless babies would seriously hamper the nomadic Dakota, and they scorned a woman who had a baby before the next older child was able to walk and care for itself.

Bison hunts could be dangerous. This Indian hunter *(upper left)* **could have been trampled if he had slipped off his galloping horse and the running bison.**

Horses became the backbone of Indian life on the Great Plains. The animals had strayed north from Spanish settlements in the 1500s.

Soon Plains Indians were much more mobile than before. On horses, they could kill more bison. Horses came to mean wealth.

The first white people to set foot in what later became Nebraska were probably Paul and Pierre Mallet. In 1739 the two brothers walked along the Platte River on their way to the Santa Fe settlement in the Southwest.

At the time, France claimed all the land between the Mississippi River and the Rocky Mountains—a huge area called Louisiana. But ownership shifted back and forth between France and Spain during the 1600s and 1700s.

Then in 1803, France sold Louisiana to the newly formed United

Platte River

States in a deal called the Louisiana Purchase. Life along the Platte River began to change fast.

The following year, Meriwether Lewis and William Clark explored the eastern edge of what would become Nebraska. In 1812 Robert Stuart started out from the Pacific coast of the Oregon Country to reach New York City, 3,000 miles (4,827 km) away. Stuart's party traveled along the Platte River and reached the Missouri River a year later. For 50 years, pioneers going to Oregon followed Stuart's route —the Oregon Trail.

In the 1700s, Plains Indians began sewing glass beads onto cloth to make colorful designs *(left)*. The Native Americans got the beads from fur traders, who operated out of trading posts *(below)*.

Fur traders began living along the Platte and Missouri rivers in 1807, when Manuel Lisa built a fur-trading post near where Omaha, Nebraska's biggest city, is now. These merchants brought metal products—arrow tips, pots, pans, axes, knives—to exchange with the Indians for furs. So the Indians stopped making their own arrowheads, pottery, and other tools.

When the traders began selling glass beads, machine-made cloth, and steel needles, Indian women quit using quills and instead sewed the traders' beads onto the traders' fabric. Indian men began to wear blankets instead of buffalo robes.

The Indians in the area knew nothing about the making or effects of alcohol. When bargaining for the finest furs, traders used whiskey to get the Indians drunk. The traders would then cheat the Indians and get rich as a result.

The fur traders also exposed Indians in the region to European diseases. In 1800 two-thirds of the Omaha died from smallpox. By 1804 three-fourths of the Ponca had, too. The Oto lost so many people to disease that the tribe never recovered.

In the early 1800s, white people called the Great Plains the Great American Desert. The region wasn't actually a desert, but few trees grew on the prairie, and not much rain fell. In fact, most white Americans agreed that the land was too poor for themselves, so they reserved it for Indians. For white people, the land along the Platte River was simply a good route to the West.

The Oregon Trail became like a highway in 1848, when a valuable yellow metal was found in California and the gold rush began. In 1850, 55,000 people crossed the Great Plains on their way to the goldfields in California. The journey to the Pacific coast took three months.

By the 1850s, some people were wanting to open the Great Plains to white settlement. To do this, the U.S. government would have to change the status of the region from Indian country to a U.S. territory. In 1854 the Kansas-Nebraska Act divided the Great Plains into the Kansas Territory to the south and the Nebraska Territory to the north.

Chimney Rock *(facing page)* **was the most famous landmark on the Oregon Trail because pioneers could see it for miles over the flat Nebraska plain.**

By the time the territory was formed, most of the Indian tribes in eastern Nebraska had already given over their lands to the U.S. government. Government officials escorted the Native Americans to **reservations**, areas of land set aside for Indian use.

But western Nebraska's Indians, such as the Sioux and Cheyenne, were reluctant to give up their lifestyles. Alarmed at the growing numbers of westbound pioneers, Indians attacked some travelers, and U.S. soldiers attacked Indians. A period known as the Indian Wars continued from 1864 to 1879, when U.S. troops crushed the last Indian fighters. With their lives shattered, the remaining Indians were forced to settle on reservations.

At this meeting in 1876, the Sioux Indians surrendered the Black Hills of South Dakota and Nebraska to the U.S. government.

Meanwhile, both the Union Pacific and the Burlington railroads tried to persuade Americans and even Europeans to come live in the Nebraska Territory. The railroads promised free land and successful farming in the territory. The more people there were in the region, the more shipping business the railroads were likely to get. The owners of the railroads would then be able to make more money.

To persuade the railroads to lay tracks across the Great Plains, the U.S. government had given the companies huge chunks of land. By 1865 railroads owned over one-seventh of Nebraska. The railroads made a fortune selling the land to settlers. U.S. citizens and European **immigrants** (newcomers) poured onto the prairie, and the railroads' owners got richer.

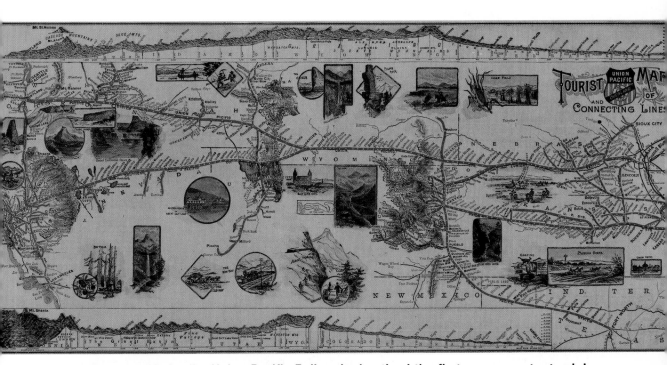

A map made by the Union Pacific Railroad advertised the first cross-country track in the United States. Travelers could view the wonders of the West from the comfort of their train car.

Immigrants to the prairie couldn't find enough trees for lumber, so people built houses made of sod. The pioneers called these blocks of earth "Nebraska marble." Worms, bugs, and snakes often fell out of the roof and into the house.

The Homestead Act encouraged still more people to come to Nebraska. Settlers could now claim 160 acres (65 hectares) of government land for free. The new residents drew up a **constitution,** and on March 1, 1867, Nebraska became the 37th state to join the Union.

The immigrants had plenty of food on the prairie. They hunted prairie chickens, jackrabbits, antelope, ducks, and deer. Lamb's-quarter, wild lettuce, asparagus, currants, chokecherries, plums, and grapes grew all around. Molasses, salt pork, and lard from the eastern United States added sugar, seasoning, and fat to the pioneers' diet.

Water was harder to find than food, though, and the land close to rivers was the first to be claimed. Some farmers hired dowsers—people who used a special stick to find water underground. There was plenty of **groundwater.** The well just had to be deep enough.

In 1873 barbed wire was invented, and farmers had a cheap way to keep animals out of their fields. Fences don't stop insects, though, and from 1874 to 1877, huge clouds of grasshoppers destroyed Nebraska's crops, even the turnips and carrots growing underground. Hard times struck again in 1886 and 1887, when harsh winters killed most of the cattle in the state.

The weather could make pioneer life difficult in the summer, too. In July 1890 the temperature rose above 100° F (38° C) for 20 days. In 1894, three scorching days wiped out almost all of the corn and wheat —the main crops.

To avoid losing everything during the next dry heat wave, Nebraskans began to **irrigate,** channeling water from the Platte River through ditches to their fields. Some farmers tried dry-land farming. This method involved carefully preparing the soil. It was covered to seal in moisture and nutrients, and different crops were grown each year. Irrigation and

dry-land farming have saved thousands of crops since the drought of the 1890s.

In the early 1900s, farmers be-

Prairie Fire!

Fire is a common threat in late summer on Nebraska's prairies. Lightning or a spark from a campfire or train wheels can easily light the dry grass, setting the plains ablaze.

The Indians taught Nebraska's settlers the only hope of protection from prairie fires—a piece of ground without grass. The flames stop at these sections of land because there is nothing to catch fire. By digging a hole in the bare ground, people could also escape the intense heat. If they had time, farmers would rush to plow a strip of land around their homes to avoid losing all their possessions.

One tragedy occurred in 1873, when a fire swept toward a schoolhouse. The teacher cautioned everyone to stay with her on a piece of bare ground, but one mother insisted on going home with some of the children. The mother and 10 children were found later. They had all died in the flames. Those who had stayed with the teacher were saved.

gan to grow sugar beets, alfalfa, and potatoes. Crop prices tripled between 1910 and 1918. In an effort to grow more and make more money, farmers borrowed money to buy more land. They spent the 1920s paying off the money they owed.

Swirling clouds of dust blocked out the sun on the Great Plains in the 1930s. The dust storms carried away rich topsoil and coated everything in their path with grime.

When drought returned to the Great Plains in the 1930s, Nebraska again looked like the Great American Desert. At night, the temperature sometimes actually rose! Huge clouds of dust darkened the sky as they swept across the plains, giving the region the nickname the Dust Bowl. Hundreds of farmers abandoned their land.

At the end of the 1930s, the rains came back to the plains. But Nebraskans had learned from the years of hardship. They sought ways to increase the size of their harvests.

For example, farmers dug more irrigation ditches to carry water to their crops. And they started using chemical fertilizers to replace nutrients that wind and irrigation water carried from the fields. Farmers also began to plant stronger kinds of corn and relied more and more on farm machinery to make their jobs easier. Crop yields increased.

For years, ranchers in western Nebraska have upheld the curious tradition of placing their boots over fence posts.

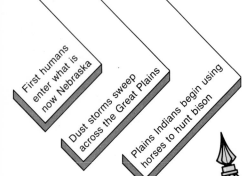

8000 B.C.   A.D. 1400   1600   1739

First humans enter what is now Nebraska

Dust storms sweep across the Great Plains

Plains Indians begin using horses to hunt bison

Paul and Pierre Mallet travel along the Platte River in Nebraska

The Nebraska flag shows a blacksmith, who stands for Nebraska's first white settlers and their hard work. Bundles of grain represent the state's agriculture.

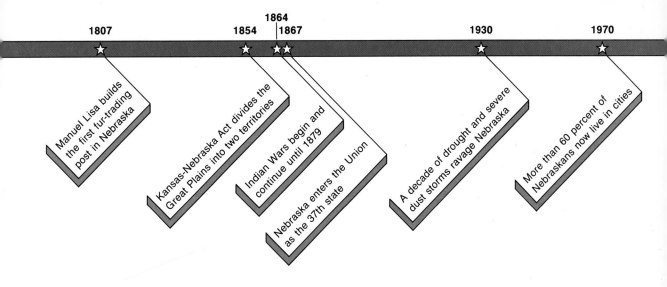

1807 — Manuel Lisa builds the first fur-trading post in Nebraska

1854 — Kansas-Nebraska Act divides the Great Plains into two territories

1864 — Indian Wars begin and continue until 1879

1867 — Nebraska enters the Union as the 37th state

1930 — A decade of drought and severe dust storms ravage Nebraska

1970 — More than 60 percent of Nebraskans now live in cities

By the 1960s and 1970s, many farm workers were moving to Nebraska's cities, since they were not needed on the mechanized farms. These Nebraskans took jobs in factories, many of which made farm equipment. Although the state has also developed other industries, its lifeblood remains agriculture.

Living and Working in Nebraska

Nebraska's 1.6 million people have close ties to their state and their fellow residents. Their ancestors came from different places, but Nebraskans have a common history of sharing Nebraska's land. And

Many Nebraskans, including this boy *(above)*, **still live in the countryside. But Omaha** *(facing page),* **Nebraska's largest city, has more than 300,000 people.**

whether they work on farms, at stores, or in factories, Nebraskans still depend on the success of agriculture. A good year for farmers means a good year for everyone.

Eastern Nebraska was the first part of the state to be plowed by early settlers, and that's where most Nebraskans still live. The main work then was farming. Now only one out of twelve Nebraskans works on a farm. And most people (63 percent) live in cities, including Omaha, Lincoln (the capital), and Grand Island—the three largest cities. But city dwellers in Nebraska still pay close attention to how well the state's farmers are doing. This is because many urban residents work in jobs that service, or help, farmers.

For example, nearly one-fourth of the state's workers sell things, including grain and cattle from Nebraska's farms. Other people transport farm products by truck, train, or river barge to markets around the country. Many farm products from Nebraska are sold throughout the world.

Most of the Nebraskans who work in factories also handle agricultural products. They cook, package, and process the crops, which are then worth more money than they were to start with.

Millworkers in Omaha, Lincoln, and Fremont grind wheat and other grains into flour for bread

A combine—a machine that gathers and cleans grain—spits wheat into a truck.

44

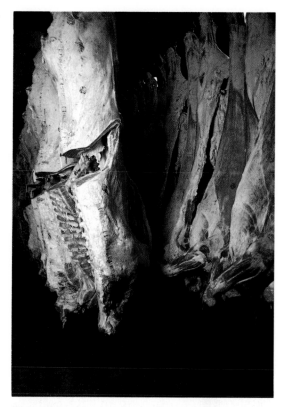

and pastries. In these three cities and in Schuyler, meat processors butcher hogs and cattle. Workers in Omaha and Lincoln make ice cream, butter, and other products from milk. The food companies that were the first in the country to turn out frozen dinners are located in Omaha.

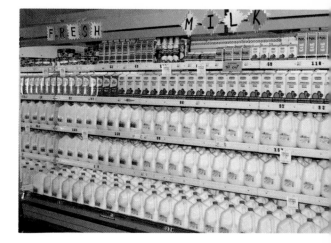

The meat *(above)* **and milk** *(right)* **of Nebraska's 5.5 million cattle are shipped to supermarkets all over the country.**

Sorghum is grown in the Platte River valley and fed to farm animals.

Farmers who irrigate their land or who live in the eastern part of the state can grow corn, sorghum, and soybeans, which need a lot of water. Nebraska's corn harvest is the third largest in the United States. After corn, hay is Nebraska's biggest crop.

Nebraska's cattle are brought to stockyards before they are sold to meat-packing plants.

Wheat, another major crop, is grown in the dry, western part of the state. This area is also where ranchers raise most of the state's beef cattle, which are worth more money than any other farm product in Nebraska.

Most of the Nebraskans who provide services to people or businesses work in or near Omaha or Lincoln. The government employs many of the people who have service jobs. Some government workers in Omaha report to Offut Air Force Base, which is the headquarters of the Strategic Air Command (SAC). During a military crisis, SAC relays the call to arms to U.S. airplanes and missile sites around the world.

Omaha hosts some other big service industries, too. For example, Mutual of Omaha is the largest private health insurance company in the world. A health insurance company promises, in exchange for regular payments, to pay for people's medical bills if they get hurt or sick.

Most of the state's small income from mining comes from oil wells in western and south central Nebraska. People who work in mines along the Platte and Republican rivers dig and sell gravel and sand for making roads and buildings.

A pump in southern Nebraska pulls oil from a well.

Almost everyone who lives in Nebraska was born in the United States. But Nebraskans represent a variety of ethnic backgrounds. In the 1800s, railroad agents persuaded many Germans to come to Nebraska, and many people of German descent still live in the state.

Other Nebraskans also have ancestors who came from Europe, including places like Czechoslovakia, Sweden, and Ireland. African Americans have lived in Nebraska, mostly in cities and towns, since the early 1800s.

On special days, these children dress in the traditional costumes of their ancestors, who came from Czechoslovakia.

Only a tiny percentage of Nebraska's Native American population survived the diseases brought to the region by European explorers. Today fewer than 3,000 Indians live on the state's three reservations—Omaha, Santee Sioux, and Winnebago.

But the lives of Indians, as well as pioneers, are remembered in some of the artworks at the Joslyn Art Museum in Omaha. And Omaha's Great Plains Black Museum details the lives of early African American cowboys, civic leaders, and other historical figures.

Omaha also features some museums devoted to children. At the Boys Town Hall of History, visitors can learn about both the hard life that some children face and the

social programs designed to help them. And the Children's Museum allows young people to try equipment for various professions, hob-

Indians on Nebraska's reservations *(facing page)* earn most of their money by selling the food they grow. During a school celebration in Boys Town *(right),* a group of children enjoys a sunny day.

bies, and other activities. For dinosaur buffs, the State Museum at the University of Nebraska in Lincoln has a fine collection of fossils and woolly-mammoth skeletons.

The Nebraska Cornhuskers are one of the best college football teams in the United States. They have won 70 percent of all their games!

The University of Nebraska also draws sports enthusiasts. When the school's football team has a Saturday game, a stadium packed with 76,000 cheering Cornhusker fans becomes the state's third largest city. Nebraskans are famed for their loyalty to this winning college team.

Nebraskans like to have fun outdoors. Several state parks offer trails for bicycling and horseback riding. And fishers, boaters, and swimmers enjoy the state's rivers and lakes.

In 1882 Buffalo Bill Cody started a Nebraskan tradition when he staged the "granddaddy of all American rodeos" in North Platte, Nebraska. A rodeo is still a favorite part of the town's yearly Ne-braskaland Days, a week of fun every June. Modern-day cowboys can also participate in numerous other rodeos held throughout the state in the summertime.

The spirit of Buffalo Bill still comes to Nebraskaland Days every June during the four-day Buffalo Bill Rodeo.

Protecting the Environment

In a state that depends as heavily on farming as Nebraska does, water is an especially important resource. The first white pioneers settled along rivers. Once that land was taken up, newcomers discovered that if they dug deep enough, they would eventually reach an underground water supply. In fact, Nebraska lies over one of the largest underground water supplies in the nation. This source of water is named the Ogallala Aquifer.

These rotating sprinklers, called irrigators, draw water from wells and spray it over crops. Water for most of Nebraska's wells comes from the Ogallala Aquifer, a natural underground storage space filled with water. This huge water supply provides water to eight states and stretches from Nebraska south across Kansas, Oklahoma, and Texas. Despite the aquifer's size, its water is being used up.

Because Nebraska does not get much rain, people pump water out of the aquifer faster than rainwater seeps back into it. Almost all of the water used in Nebraska's homes and businesses comes from the ground. Farmers pump huge quantities to irrigate their fields.

Residents have also drawn from surface water supplies, channeling water from the Platte and other rivers to farms and communities. As Nebraskans use up more and more of the state's water supplies, animals and plants that depend on this resource become threatened.

For example, the Platte River is part of the Central Flyway, a route used by millions of migratory birds each spring and fall. These birds, which include ducks, geese, and

Water gushes from pipes to flood a field. Fewer farmers are using this method of irrigation because much of the water is wasted.

A flock of migrating geese settles on a pond in the Rainwater Basin.

sandhill cranes, now have a much smaller area to rest and feed in than they once did.

In the past, worms, snakes, frogs, and snails—food for the cranes—lived on vast plains that stretched along the Platte. Farmers now plow, weed, and fertilize fields that line the Platte's banks, and cranes have difficulty getting enough food for the rest of their migration.

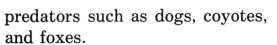

Dams in neighboring states cut down the flow of the Platte River by two-thirds before it even reaches Nebraska. So the Platte isn't nearly as wide as it used to be. Sandhill cranes can find only two resting places that are safe from predators such as dogs, coyotes, and foxes.

Other places in Nebraska also suffer from a depleted water supply. The Rainwater Basin in south central Nebraska is drying up. For millions of years, rainwater and

floodwaters from the Platte River have formed marshes in the basin, where many animals live.

In the 1900s, however, farmers have drained over four-fifths of the Rainwater Basin's original area. Under a law made in 1936, the U.S. government paid up to one-half of the cost of draining wetlands.

With less water, birds and other marsh animals must crowd together. The added stress on ducks and geese causes thousands of birds to die each year of fowl cholera.

At the Children's Ground-water Festival in Grand Island, students learn the importance of conserving water.

Various organizations in Nebraska are working to preserve the state's water supplies. Farmers have learned how to grow crops with less water. But some farmers resist efforts to save wetlands for wildlife. They say that wetlands are more valuable once they have been drained for farming because of the money that crops can earn.

Other Nebraskans, however, point out that by preserving wetlands, the state can earn money from visitors who come to view wildlife. And preserving water supplies is important for humans in the state, too. If Nebraskans continue to use water faster than nature can restock it, then one day none will be left.

All Nebraskans can help to conserve water. For example, people can take shorter showers, sprinkle the lawn for less time, turn off the faucet while brushing their teeth. By doing these things, Nebraskans can help not only wildlife but also their own future generations.

Nebraska's Famous People

ACTIVISTS & LEADERS

Edward Joseph Flanagan (1886–1948), a Roman Catholic priest, was born in Ireland. He founded Father Flanagan's Home for Boys in Omaha. The home became Boys Town in 1922. More than 8,500 mistreated and handicapped boys and girls are helped every year in Boys Town.

Malcolm X (Malcolm Little) (1925–1965), a civil rights leader who was born in Omaha, taught pride in the achievements of black people. He led a movement to unite black people all over the world and believed that blacks should have a separate nation. He was assassinated on February 21, 1965.

Julius Sterling Morton (1832–1902) moved to Nebraska when he was 22 years old. He began planting trees around his treeless yard and town. He even founded a special day for planting trees, Arbor Day, which has become a national holiday.

▲ MALCOLM X

▲ EDWARD JOSEPH FLANAGAN

JULIUS STERLING MORTON ▶

MARLON ▼ BRANDO

Susan LaFlesche Picotte (1865–1915) was the first Native American woman to earn a medical degree. She devoted her life to improving Indian health care on the Omaha Reservation in northeastern Nebraska, where she grew up.

ACTORS

Marlon Brando (born 1924) is from Omaha. An actor, Brando has won Academy Awards for his films *On the Waterfront* and

▲ SUSAN LaFLESCHE PICOTTE

The Godfather. Brando is known for his rough, slurred speech and for his bulky, powerful body.

Henry Jaynes Fonda (1905–1982) was an actor born in Grand Island, Nebraska. Since the 1930s, Fonda appeared in more than 80 films, including *The Grapes of Wrath, Mister Roberts,* and *On Golden Pond,* for which he won an Oscar in 1981.

Robert Taylor (1911–1969), a Hollywood film star, was named Arlington Spangler Brugh when he was born in Filley, Nebraska. Taylor's good looks and charm attracted crowds to his films from the 1930s through the 1950s.

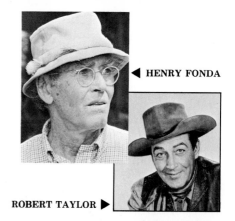

◀ HENRY FONDA

ROBERT TAYLOR ▶

WADE BOGGS ▶

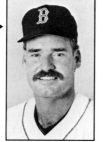

ATHLETES

Wade Boggs (born 1958) comes from Omaha. A baseball infielder for the Boston Red Sox since 1982, Boggs has won several American League batting titles.

Bob Gibson (born 1935) was a pitcher for the St. Louis Cardinals from 1959 to 1975. Born in Omaha, Gibson twice won the Cy Young Award for best pitcher of the year in the National League. In 1981 he was admitted to the Baseball Hall of Fame.

ENTERTAINERS

Fred Astaire (1899–1987) danced and acted with a style that made him world famous. Astaire was born in Omaha and began his career dancing with his sister Adele. He appeared in more than 30 film musicals, including 10 with his famous dance partner, Ginger Rogers.

◀ FRED ASTAIRE

Johnny Carson (born 1925) began performing at a young age, putting on magic shows and acting in plays. Born in Iowa, Carson grew up in Norfolk, Nebraska. He got his first broadcasting job in Lincoln. He has hosted "The Tonight Show" since 1962.

William Frederick ("Buffalo Bill") Cody (1846–1917) started his career as a field hand when he was nine. He went on to become a scout, buffalo hunter, showman, Pony Express rider, and actor. A native of Iowa, Buffalo Bill staged the first American rodeo in North Platte, Nebraska.

◀ JOHNNY CARSON

BUFFALO BILL ▶

◀ RED CLOUD

INDIAN LEADERS

Crazy Horse (Tashunca-uitco) (1844?–1877), an Oglala Sioux chief, tried to recapture Indian lands from the United States. He led his people in raids on white settlements and warred against U.S. Army troops. Crazy Horse was killed while being forced into a jail cell in Camp Robinson, Nebraska.

Red Cloud (Makhpíya-Lúta) (1822–1909) was a war leader for the Oglala Sioux. Born in Nebraska, Red Cloud tried to stop the opening of the Bozeman Trail, which ran through Indian hunting grounds in Wyoming and Montana. He eventually signed a peace treaty and lived on a reservation named for him.

POLITICIANS

WILLIAM ▶
JENNINGS
BRYAN

William Jennings Bryan (1860–1925) moved to Lincoln in 1887 and served as a representative from Nebraska in the U.S. Congress. He ran for president three times, but he never won. Known as one of the greatest speakers of his time, Bryan worked to improve the lives of farmers and influenced people all over the nation.

George William Norris (1861–1944), a native of Ohio, represented Nebraska in the U.S. Congress for 40 years. He convinced the government to provide electricity to rural areas. He also gave money to Nebraska's farmers in times of drought.

◄ **GEORGE WILLIAM NORRIS**

◄ **C. W. ANDERSON**

WRITERS

Clarence William (C. W.) Anderson (1891–1971) was an author who also illustrated books about horses. Born in Wahoo, Nebraska, he became famous for his *Billy and Blaze* series. Anderson's own first horse, Bobcat, was a model for some of the horses in the books.

Willa Sibert Cather (1873–1947), an author, moved from Virginia to Nebraska at the age of 10. Several of her novels tell of the pioneer Midwest, including *O Pioneers!* and *My Antonia.* The novel *One of Ours* won Cather a Pulitzer Prize in 1923.

Mari Sandoz (1900–1966), born in Sheridan County, Nebraska, played with many Indians as a child. She wrote about the lives of Indians, ranchers, and homesteaders in *Love Song to the Plains,* a history of Nebraska. She also wrote two children's books about Sioux life, *The Horse Catcher* and *The Story Catcher.*

WILLA CATHER ▶

65

Facts-at-a-Glance

Nickname: Cornhusker State
Song: "Beautiful Nebraska"
Motto: Equality Before the Law
Flower: goldenrod
Tree: cottonwood
Bird: western meadowlark

Population: 1,588,000 (1990 estimate)
Rank in population, nationwide: 37th
Area: 77,355 sq mi (200,350 sq km)
Rank in area, nationwide: 15th
Date and ranking of statehood:
  March 1, 1867, the 37th state
Capital: Lincoln
Major cities (and populations*):
  Omaha (313,939), Lincoln (171,932), Grand
  Island (33,180), North Platte (24,509), Fremont
  (23,979)
U.S. senators: 2
U.S. representatives: 3
Electoral votes: 5

Places to visit: Agate Fossil Beds National Monument in northwestern Nebraska, Boys Town near Omaha, Buffalo Bill's home near North Platte, Chimney Rock National Historic Site near Bayard, Toadstool Park near Crawford

Annual events: National Indoor Truck and Tractor Pull in Omaha (Jan.), Arbor Day (April), German Heritage Festival in McCook (May), Nebraska's Biggest Rodeo in Burwell (August), Husker Harvest Days in Grand Island (Sept.)

* 1986 estimates

Average January temperature: 23° F (–5° C)	Average July temperature: 76° F (25° C)

Natural resources: soil, water, limestone, sand, gravel, clay, petroleum, natural gas

Agricultural products: corn, hay, soybeans, sorghum, wheat, beef cattle, hogs, milk, beans, potatoes, sugar beets

Manufactured goods: food products, machinery, chemicals, electrical equipment, metal products

ENDANGERED SPECIES

Mammals—river otter, black-footed ferret, swift fox

Birds—bald eagle, least tern, interior whooping crane, American peregrine falcon, Arctic peregrine falcon, Eskimo curlew

Insects—American burying beetle

Plants—Hayden penstemon

WHERE NEBRASKANS WORK
Services—54 percent
   (services includes jobs in trade; community, social, & personal services; finance, insurance, & real estate; transportation, communication, & utilities)
Government—18 percent
Agriculture—12 percent
Manufacturing—12 percent
Construction—4 percent

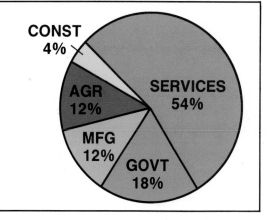

CONST 4%
AGR 12%
SERVICES 54%
MFG 12%
GOVT 18%

Apache (uh-PACH-ee)

Cheyenne (shy-AN)

Czechoslovakia
(chehk-uh-sloh-VAHK-ee-uh)

Loup (LOOP)

McConaughy (muh-KAHN-uh-hay)

Mallet, Pierre (mah-LAY, pee-AIR)

Niobrara (ny-uh-BRAHR-uh)

Ogallala Aquifer
(oh-guh-LAHL-uh AK-weh-fur)

Oto (OHD-oh)

Pawnee (paw-NEE)

Platte (PLAT)

Ponca (PAHNG-kuh)

Sioux (SOO)

Glossary

constitution The system of basic laws or rules of a government, society, or organization. The document in which these laws or rules are written.

drought A long period of extreme dryness due to lack of rain or snow.

glacier A large body of ice and snow that moves slowly over land.

groundwater Water that lies beneath the earth's surface. The water comes from rain and snow that seep through soil into the cracks and other openings in rocks. Groundwater supplies wells and springs.

hydropower The electricity produced by using waterpower. Also called hydro-electric power.

immigrant A person who moves into a foreign country and settles there.

irrigate To water land by directing water through canals, ditches, pipes, or sprinklers.

loess Fine-grained soil or dust that is carried by wind and deposited on the ground.

marshland A spongy wetland soaked with water for long periods of time. Marshland is usually treeless; grasses are the main form of vegetation found in marshland.

prairie A large area of level or gently rolling grassy land with few trees.

reservation Public land set aside by the government to be used by Native Americans.

till A mixture of clay, sand, and gravel dragged along by a glacier and left behind when the ice melts.

Index

Acknowledgments:

Maryland Cartographics, Inc., pp. 2, 11; John Cunningham / Visuals Unlimited, pp. 2-3, 21, 26 (left); National Museum of Roller Skating, p. 6; Jack Lindstrom, p. 7; U.S. Fish and Wildlife Service, pp. 8, 57, 58-59 (Alan Trout); Nebraska Game and Parks, p. 9, 54; Mary M. Tremaine / Root Resources, p. 12; Kent & Donna Dannen, pp. 13, 16, 17 (left and right), 39, 55 (bottom), 61; Merrilee Thomas, p. 14; Stan Strange / Root Resources, p. 15; National Park Service, p. 18; Smithsonian Institution photo #80-1819, p. 19; Lincoln Convention and Visitors Bureau, p. 20; Independent Picture Service, pp. 23, 65 (bottom); Nebraska Natural Resources Commission, Terry L. Cartwright, photographer, pp. 24-25, 56; Nebraska Department of Economic Development, pp. 26 (right), 42, 53, 71; Harper's Weekly, November 2, 1867, Oregon Historical Society, OrHi 23551, p. 29; Jeff Greenberg, pp. 30, 50; Nebraska State Historical Society, pp. 31, 36-37, 62 (center, bottom left), 64 (top right), 65 (top); Union Pacific Museum Collection, pp. 32, 33; Solomon P. Butcher Collection, Nebraska State Historical Society, p. 34; R. Culentine / Visuals Unlimited, p. 35; Library of Congress, pp. 38, 64 (bottom); Laura Westlund, p. 40; Phyllis Cerny, pp. 43, 55 (top); Doyen Salsig, pp. 44, 46, 47 (left); M. Long / Visuals Unlimited, p. 45 (left); Roberts Dairy Company, Omaha, NE, p. 45 (right); Steve Cathcart, Southwest Nebraska Convention and Visitors Bureau, p. 48; Lambert Slepicka, p. 49; Boys Town, pp. 51, 62 (top left); University of Nebraska, p. 52; William J. Weber / Visuals Unlimited, pp. 58 (left), 59 (right); Tom J. Ulrich / Visuals Unlimited, p. 58 (center); Nebraska Department of Environmental Control, p. 60; Wide World, p. 62 (top right); Hollywood Book & Poster Co., pp. 62 (bottom right), 63 (top left, top right, bottom left), 64 (top left); Boston Red Sox, p. 63 (center); Smithsonian Institution National Anthropological Archives, Bureau of American Ethnology Collection, p. 64 (center, neg. #3237-A); MacMillan Publishing Company, p. 65 (center); Jean Matheny, p. 66; Kenneth W. Fink / Root Resources, p. 69